SONGS OF CAT STEV

WISE PUBLICATIONS
NEW YORK/LONDON/SYDNEY

EXCLUSIVE DISTRIBUTORS
MUSIC SALES CORPORATION
257 PARK AVENUE SOUTH, NEW YORK, NY 10010 USA
MUSIC SALES LIMITED
8/9 FRITH STREET, LONDON W1V 5TZ ENGLAND
MUSIC SALES PTY. LIMITED
120 ROTHSCHILD STREET, ROSEBERY, SYDNEY, NSW 2018, AUSTRALIA

THIS BOOK COPYRIGHT © 1983 BY WISE PUBLICATIONS
ISBN 0.7119.0289.5 ORDER NO. AM 32954

COVER PHOTOGRAPH BY L.F.I.
COMPILED BY PETER EVANS

MUSIC SALES COMPLETE CATALOGUE LISTS THOUSANDS OF TITLES AND IS FREE
FROM YOUR LOCAL MUSIC SHOP, OR DIRECT FROM MUSIC SALES LIMITED.
PLEASE SEND 50P IN STAMPS FOR POSTAGE TO MUSIC SALES LIMITED,
8/9 FRITH STREET, LONDON W1V 5TZ

PRINTED IN THE UNITED STATES OF AMERICA BY
VICKS LITHOGRAPH AND PRINTING CORPORATION

ANOTHER SATURDAY NIGHT

WORDS & MUSIC BY SAM COOKE

BITTERBLUE

WORDS & MUSIC BY CAT STEVENS

Brite Rock

I gave my last chance to you don't hand it back to me Bit-ter Blue

I gave my last hope to you don't hand it back to me Bit-ter Blue

No Bit-ter Blue

My Bit-ter Blue

8

D. S. al Coda

CODA

I gave my last_____ chance to you don't hand it back to me Bit-ter Blue_

My Bit-ter Blue

I've done all one_ man can do_ don't pass me up_ Oh Bit-ter Blue_

BUT I MIGHT DIE TONIGHT

WORDS & MUSIC BY CAT STEVENS

Slowly

Don't want   to work a - way   do - in' just what they all say.

Work hard boy   you'll find   one day___ you'll have a   job like mine.___

'Cause I know   for   sure   no - bod — y should be that poor.

To say yes____ or sink__ low be-cause you hap-pen to say so, say so,

You say so, I don't want to work a - way.

do - in' just what they all say. work hard boy you'll find

one day__ you'll have a job like mine, job like mine. A job like mine

13

be wise___ look a-head___ use your eyes,___ he said,

Be straight, think right, but I might die to-night.___

Aah.___

CAN'T KEEP IT IN

WORDS & MUSIC BY CAT STEVENS

love that's in me. I said, why walk a-lone, why wor-ry when it's warm o-ver here.

You've got so much to say, say——— what you mean, mean what you're think-ing and think———

——— an-y-thing. Oh why,——————— why must you

waste your life— a-way,——— you've got to live for to-day,——— then let it go.———

Oh _____ · lov - er,

I want to spend this time with — you, _____ there's no-thing I would-n't do—

_____ if you let me know. _____ And I Can't-

— Keep It In, I can't hide it and I can't lock it a-way. I'm up-

for your love, love —— heats my blood, blood spins my head and my head —— falls in love, oh.

No I Can't —

— Keep It In, I Can't Keep It In, I've got-ta let it out.

I've got-ta show the world, world's _____ got-ta know,

know of the love, love _____ that lies low, so why can't you say,

if you know then why can't you say. You've got too much de-ceit, de-ceit ____

____ kills the light, light _____ needs to shine, I said shine _____ light, shine light,

love. _____ _____ That's no way to live your life, _____

_____ you al-low too much to go by, _____ and that won't do, _____

no _____ lov-er.

I want to have you here by — my side, now don't you

FATHER AND SON

WORDS & MUSIC BY CAT STEVENS

23

still be here tomorrow but your dreams may not.   How can

I try to ex-plain?   When I   do   he turns a-way___ a-gain,   It's

al-ways been the same, same old sto-ry.   From the   mo-ment I could talk   I was

or-dered to lis-ten now there's a   way_____   and I   know that I

THE FIRST CUT IS THE DEEPEST

WORDS & MUSIC BY CAT STEVENS

The first cut is the deep - est; ba - by, I know___ the first cut is the deep -

est. When it comes to be - in' luck - y she's cursed;___ when it

1.

comes to lov - in' me she's worse.___ I still

2.

Repeat and fade

comes to lov - in' me she's worse.___

Repeat and fade

HARD HEADED WOMAN

WORDS & MUSIC BY CAT STEVENS

I'm look-ing for a hard headed wom-an   One who'll make me do__ my

to Coda ⊕

best,__   And if I find my hard head-ed wom - an.__

I know the rest of my life__ will be blessed, yes, yes, yes.__

I know a lot of fan - cy danc - ers   Peo-ple who can glide you__ on a

floor,_____ They move so smooth ___ but have no ans-wers__

when you ask _____ why'd you come here for?

(spoken)
Why?
(I don't know)

I know man - y fine feath-ered friends_____ but their
They know man - y sure fired ways _____ to find

friend- li- ness de- pends _____ on how you do.__
out the one who pays _____ and how you do.__

I'm look- ing for a hard head-ed wom - an,

one who will make me feel so good, And if I find my hard head-ed

wom- an I know my life will be as it should, yes yes, yes.

Coda

I THINK I SEE THE LIGHT

WORDS & MUSIC BY CAT STEVENS

I used to trust no-body, trust-ing e-ven less their words,__

un-til I found some-body, there was no one I pre-ferred.__
My heart was made of stone, my eyes saw on-ly mis-ty grey.__

Un-til you came in-to my life girl, I saw ev-'ry-one that way.___
Un-til you came in-to my life girl, I saw noth-ing, noth-ing more.___

Un-til I found the one I need-ed at my side,

I think I would have been a sad man all my life.___

I think I see the light___ com-ing to me,___ com-ing

through me___ giv-ing me a sec-ond___ sight,___ so

shine___ shine___ shine   shine___ shine___ shine

shine   shine   shine._____

I used to walk a- lone,___ ev-'ry step seemed the same,___

This world was not my home___ so there was noth-ing much to gain,___
Look up and see the clouds___ look down and see the cold___ floor,___

1. | 2. D.S. al Coda | CODA

I think I see the light___ coming to___ me,___ com-ing

thru me,_____ Giv-ing me a sec-ond___ sight.___ So

shine___ shine___ shine shine___ shine___ shine.

Repeat
5 times

MAYBE YOU'RE RIGHT

WORDS & MUSIC BY CAT STEVENS

1. Now may-be you're right
2. So may-be you're right

and may-be you're wrong

But I ain't gon-na ar-gue with you no more I've done it for too long.

It was get-ting so good why then where did it go___ I can't

think a-bout it no more, tell me if___ you know,_____ You were loving

me, I_____ was lov-ing you___ But now there aint no-thing but regretting

no-thing,___ no-thing but re-gret-ting ev-'ry-thing we do,_____

to Coda ⊕

I put up __ with your lies like __ you put up with mine, __ But God knows we

should have stopped some-where, __ we could have tak-en the time, _____ But time has

39

hap-pen a-gain,___   Nev-er,   nev-er,_nev-er,   It - 'll nev-er hap-pen a-gain___

No, no, no, no, no,_____   no,   no,   no,   no,   no.

D.S. al ⊕ Coda

CODA

pp

LADY D'ARBANVILLE

WORDS & MUSIC BY CAT STEVENS

and you will be my fill, Yes, you will be my fill. My

La-dy d'Ar-ban-ville why does it grieve me so?

But your heart seems so si-lent. Why

do you breathe so low why do you breathe so low, my La-dy d'Ar-ban-ville
2. I loved you my la-dy

La - dy d'Ar - ban - ville   you look so cold to - night,

Your lips feel like win - ter,   Your

skin' has turned to white, your skin has turned to white. My La- dy d'Ar-ban-ville

why do you sleep so still,   I'll

wake you to - mor - row   And you will be my fill, Yes,

you will be my fill. La, la, la, la, la, la.   La,

la, la, la, la, la.   La, la, la, la, la, la, la.

La, la, la, la, la, la,   la, la, la, la, la, la.

MONA BONE JAKON

WORDS & MUSIC BY CAT STEVENS

Brightly

Yes, I've got a Mon - a Bone Ja - kon, _____ But it won't be lone - ly for long. Yes, I've got a Mon - a Bone Ja - kon, _____ But it won't be lone - ly

MOONSHADOW

WORDS & MUSIC BY CAT STEVENS

52

Em7 A7 G F#m Em F#m Em A7
I won't beg, yes if I ev - er lose my legs, Oh if
north or south, yes if I ev - er lose my mouth, Oh if
D F#m Bm 1. Em A7 D 2. Em A7
I won't have to walk any more and
I won't have to talk.
D G D D A7 D
E7 A E A
Did it take long to find me? I asked the faith - ful light.
f

Did it take long to find ___ me ___ and are you gon-na stay the night. ___ Oh

I'm be-in' fol-lowed by a moon shad-ow, moon shad-ow, moon shad-ow, ___

leap-in' and hop-in' on a moon shad-ow, moon shad-ow, moon shad-ow, ___

moon shad-ow, moon shad-ow, ___ moon shad-ow, moon shad-ow. ___

MORNING HAS BROKEN

WORDS BY ELEANOR FARJEON
MUSICAL ARRANGEMENT BY CAT STEVENS

a tempo

mp

3. Mine is the sun - light, Mine is the morn -

ing, Born of the one light E - den saw play.

Praise with e - la - tion, Praise ev-'ry morn -

ing, God's re - cre - a - tion of the new day.

mf

SAD LISA

WORDS & MUSIC BY CAT STEVENS

must   be._____
near   me._____
see   her._____

Li- sa, Li - sa_____   sad   Li- sa, Li- sa._____

1.2.3.
                                                2. Her
                                                3. (Instrumental)
                                                4. She

4.

61

TEA FOR THE TILLERMAN

WORDS & MUSIC BY CAT STEVENS

Faster

sin - ners sin the child - ren play,_____

Oh, Lord_____ how they play and play,_____ for that

hap - py day_____ for that hap - py day._____

63

TUESDAY'S DEAD

WORDS & MUSIC BY CAT STEVENS

Fairly Bright Jamaican (in 2)

If I make a mark in time, I can't say the mark is mine. I'm on-ly the un-

told to-mor-row Tues - day's dead.

2. Oh, Now

ev - 'ry sec - ond on the nose the hum-drum of the ci-ty grows,

reach - ing out be-yond the throes of our time.

66

We must try___ to shake it down, Do our best___ to break the ground,

try to turn___ the world a - round one more

time.___

2nd time
D.S. al Coda

⊕ *CODA*

Tues - day's dead.___

Oh preacher won't you paint my dream
won't you show me where you've been,
show me what I haven't seen
to ease my mind
'Cause I will learn to understand
If I have a helping hand
I wouldn't make another demand, all my life
Whoa - where do you go when you don't
want no-one to know
Who told tomorrow - Tuesday's dead

What's my sex, what's my name,
all in all it's all the same
everybody plays a different game - that is all
Now man may live, man may die
searching for the question why,
but if he tries to rule the sky - he must fall
Whoa - where do you go when you don't
want no-one to know
Who told tomorrow - Tuesday's dead
Now every second on the nose
The humdrum of the city grows

PEACE TRAIN

WORDS & MUSIC BY CAT STEVENS

out on — the edge — of dark-ness — there rides — a peace train. Oh,

peace train — take — this coun-try, come take — me home — a-gain. Now

I've been — smil - in' late-ly — think-in' a - bout the good things — to come,

and I — be-lieve — it could — be. Some-thing — good has be-gun. Oh,

Get your __ bags __ to-geth-er __ go bring your good friends __ too. Be-

cause it's __ get - tin' near - er __ it soon __ will be with you. Oh

come and __ join the liv - ing __ it's not __ so far from you. Oh

and it's __ get - tin' near - er soon it __ will all __ be true. Oh

Peace Train sound - ing loud-er   glide on _ the Peace   Train   OO _____

_____   come on _ now Peace   Train, Peace Train.

Now

I've   been _ cry - in' late-ly _   think-in' a - bout   the world   as   it   is

why must _we go ___ on hat - ing   why can't _we live in   bliss.   'Cause

out   on _ the edge of dark - ness ___   there rides _a Peace   Train   Oh

D.S. al Coda

Peace   Train _ take ___ this coun - try   come take _me home ___ a - gain.   Oh

Coda

come   on _ Peace ___ Train   yes it's _ the Peace   Train!

LONGER BOATS

WORDS & MUSIC BY CAT STEVENS

tak - ing the key _____ from the door.

Fine

J don't
Ma - ry

want, no, God _____ on my lawn _____ _____ just a
dropped her pants _____ by the sand _____ _____ and let a

flow - er I can help a - long _____ 'Cause the
par - son come and take her hand _____ But the

WILD WORLD

WORDS & MUSIC BY CAT STEVENS

1. Now that I've lost ev-'ry-thing to you _____ you say you wan- na start some-thing new_
2. You know I've seen a lot of what the world can do _____ and it's break-ing my heart in two_

_____ and it's break-ing my heart _ you're leav- ing. Ba- by. I'm griev - in'!
_____ be-cause I nev - er want to see you sad, girl. Don't be a bad _ girl.

But if you want to leave take good care, hope you have a lot of nice things to wear_
But if you want to leave take good care, hope you make a lot of nice friends out there_

but then a lot of nice things turn bad out there. ___
but just re-mem-ber there's a lot of bad and be-ware. ___

Oh ba-by, ba - by it's a WILD WORLD.   It's hard to get by ___ just up-on a

smile.   Oh, ba-by, ba - by it's a WILD WORLD.

to Coda

I'll al-ways re-mem - ber you ___ like a child girl. ___

child, girl.____

Ba-by I love__ you,   But if you want to leave_take good

care, hope you make a lot of nice friends out there. But just re-mem-ber there's a lot of bad

and be-ware____

child, girl.____